# Perfect Food for Babies and Toddlers

### Delicious and nutritious recipes for your children

First published in 2010
LOVE FOOD is an imprint of Parragon Books Ltd

Parragon
Queen Street House
4 Queen Street
Bath BA1 1HE, UK

ISBN: 978-1-4454-1635-9

Printed in China

Text: Valerie Barrett
New photography: Clive Bozzard-Hill
Home economist: Valerie Barrett
Cover and internal design: Sarah Knight

NOTES FOR THE READER
This book uses imperial, metric, and US cup measurements. Follow the same units of measurement throughout; do not mix imperial and metric. All spoon measurements are level: teaspoons are assumed to be 5 ml, and tablespoons are assumed to be 15 ml. Unless otherwise stated, milk is assumed to be whole, eggs and individual vegetables, such as potatoes, are medium, and pepper is freshly ground black pepper.

The times given are an approximate guide only. Preparation times differ according to the techniques used by different people and the cooking times may also vary from those given as a result of the type of oven used. Optional ingredients, variations, or serving suggestions have not been included in the calculations.

Recipes using raw or very lightly cooked eggs should be avoided by infants, the elderly, pregnant women, convalescents, and anyone with a chronic condition. Pregnant and breast-feeding women are advised to avoid eating peanuts and peanut products. People with nut allergies should be aware that some of the prepared ingredients used in the recipes in this book may contain nuts. Always check the package before use.

PICTURE ACKNOWLEDGEMENTS
The publisher would like to thank the following for permission to reproduce copyright material
Front cover image: Girl Sitting at Table Holding Spoon © Dave King/Getty Images

# Contents

# Introduction

Creating a happy and healthy home environment where a child can grow and thrive is every parent's aim. Food plays a major part in this, because good health stems from good nutrition. This book will give you information about nutrition, advice on feeding your baby from weaning to preschool, and recipes and tips that will help you make delicious everyday meals your child will enjoy.

When babies are born, we always wish them good health and happiness. As a parent you can lay the foundation for a lifetime of good health by making sure they have a well-balanced, nutritious diet and that they establish good eating habits. A good diet will reduce their risk of developing certain illnesses both in childhood and in adult life.

The first few years of parenthood are a roller-coaster journey of discovery and learning. No sooner have you mastered the art of breast- or bottle-feeding than it's suddenly time to introduce solids. As a first-time parent this is all new and somewhat scary. Armed with a little helpful information and a few good tips and recipes, however, you will find it is really straightforward.

As for the second wish—happiness—a healthy, well-fed child is certain to be a happy child, too. Happiness comes from feeling part of a family and being together. Mealtimes are about more than just food—they are about sharing and bonding with family members. With life today being so hectic, it is easy to slip into the habit of eating on the go or at different times, depending on everyone's needs. By sharing a meal, your baby will watch and copy you and so learn how to hold a spoon, how to eat, and how to behave. By cooking the food yourself, you will know that everything your baby or toddler eats is fresh and nutritious.

## MAKING THE RIGHT CHOICES

Nutrition is a very complicated science and babies and children have very different needs from adults. You may not spend much time thinking about your own nutrition, but you certainly need to consider that of your child. This may well lead you to think more about what you eat—especially if you have been through a pregnancy, you will have already started to do this. So the first step is to think about your own diet, because within a couple of years your child will be eating along with you.

## CARBOHYDRATES

There are two main types of carbohydrates: complex (or starchy) carbohydrates—found in potatoes, rice, pasta, bread, and cereals—and simple (or refined) carbohydrates, such as sugar. Both types are turned into glucose in the body, which in turn is then used for energy. Complex carbohydrates are a good source of vitamins, minerals, and fiber, and they release energy slowly over a long period of time. Refined carbohydrates provide calories but no nutrients. They are turned into glucose very rapidly, producing a short-lived energy "burst" which is followed by an energy "low." Because refined sugar is cheap and tastes good, it is added to many manufactured foods.

## FAT

Fat is an essential nutrient, which protects internal organs and keeps tissue healthy. Fat contains a lot of calories in a small volume and is a very concentrated source of energy. This is good for babies, who require a lot of calories but have small stomachs. Babies and toddlers should not be given a low-fat diet.

## VITAMINS AND MINERALS

Vitamins support the immune system, help the brain function, and help convert food into energy. They are needed for healthy skin and hair, controlling growth, and balancing hormones. Vitamins are only required in small amounts and can be found in a wide variety of foods. There are two types: fat-soluble vitamins A, D, E, and K, which can be stored in the body, and water-soluble vitamin C and B group vitamins, which need to be taken daily in the diet and which are destroyed by cooking. Minerals are inorganic substances needed for a range of body functions. There are many minerals that we need, the two most important for children being calcium and iron.

## PROTEINS

Proteins are made up of amino acids and are essential for the building and repair of all cells and tissues in the body. Proteins from animal foods contain all of the essential amino acids, while those from vegetables tend to be low in one or more. Most people get enough protein in their diet, but vegans and vegetarians need to eat a very varied diet to ensure they get enough protein. Children need more protein in relation to their size than adults do, so it is important to make sure they get enough.

## FIBER

High-fiber foods are too bulky and filling for babies. They are also too low in calories. Your baby will get enough fiber from fruits and vegetables.

# Weaning Plan

Over the months, the amount of food your baby takes will increase gradually.
Don't be tempted to rush, but be guided by your baby's appetite.

| | ON WAKING | BREAKFAST | LUNCH | TEA | EVENING |
|---|---|---|---|---|---|
| Stage 1 (around 6 months) | Breast-or bottle-feed | Infant rice mixed with baby's usual milk (1–2 teaspoons); breast- or bottle-feed | Breast-or bottle-feed | Breast-or bottle-feed | Breast-or bottle-feed |
| Stage 2 (around 6½ months) | Breast-or bottle-feed | Infant rice mixed with baby's usual milk; breast- or bottle-feed | 1 or 2 teaspoons pureed vegetables or fruit; breast- or bottle-feed | Breast-or bottle-feed | Breast-or bottle-feed |
| Stage 3 (around 7–8 months) | Breast-or bottle-feed | Infant rice with pureed fruit; breast- or bottle-feed | Pureed chicken or fish with vegetables; cooled boiled water to drink | Pureed vegetables or fruit; breast- or bottle-feed | Breast-or bottle-feed |
| Stage 4 (around 8–10 months) | Breast-or bottle-feed | Infant rice or porridge or other baby breakfast cereal with milk or water and pureed fruit; breast- or bottle-feed | Pureed or mashed meat, chicken or fish, with beans or lentils or potatoes or rice or pasta and vegetables; slices of fruit; cooled boiled water or well-diluted juice | Yogurt with chopped, pureed, or stewed fruit; slices of toast or bread sticks and savory dips; breast- or bottle-feed | Breast- or bottle-feed, if required |
| Stage 5 (around 10–12 months) | Babies may or may not need milk on waking, but they may be thirsty, so offer water or well-diluted fruit juice. | Porridge or breakfast cereal with fresh fruit; slices of toast; breast- or bottle-feed | Chopped meat, chicken or fish, with beans, lentils, rice, pasta, potatoes, or bread and vegetables; slices of fruit and/or yogurt or milk dessert; water or well-diluted juice | Pasta dish or soup; bread or slices of toast; fresh fruit; breast- or bottle-feed | Breast- or bottle-feed, if required |

Continue to offer breast- or bottle-feeds between meals if your baby wants them, but as meals become more established, you will find that your baby will need less of these. Offer small healthy snacks if your baby is incredibly active, because this will keep up energy levels.

# Introducing Foods into your Baby's Diet

| FOOD | 4–6 MONTHS | 6 MONTHS+ | 8 MONTHS+ | 10 MONTHS+ | 1 YEAR+ | NOTE |
|---|---|---|---|---|---|---|
| Vegetables | Cooked purees | Cooked purees and mashed | Cooked purees and sticks | Cooked and raw sticks | | |
| Fruit | Cooked purees | Cooked purees and mashed. Some raw fruits, such as banana | Add some finger foods toward the end of this stage | Cooked and raw finger foods | | |
| Cow's milk and dairy | No | No, but can add cooked milk and yogurt at the end of this stage | Add mild hard cheeses and other dairy products | | Introduce whole milk to drink | Lowfat milk may be introduced after 2 years if your baby is healthy and has a varied diet |
| Meat and chicken | No | No, but can be introduced toward the end of this stage | Start with chicken and gradually introduce red meat. No offal until over 1 year and then only tiny amounts | | | |
| Bacon and ham | No | No | Can be introduced in small amounts only as high in salt | | | |
| Fish | No | No, but white fish can be introduced toward the end of this stage | | Small amounts of oily fish such as tuna and salmon | A variety of fish can be served but children should not have shark, marlin, or swordfish | |
| Smoked fish and shellfish | No | No | No | No | In moderation and well-cooked | If risk of allergy, wait until 3 or 4 years |
| Eggs | No | Well-cooked, yolk only | Well-cooked, whole egg, if no risk of allergy | Well-cooked, whole egg, if no risk of allergy | Well-cooked, whole egg | If risk of allergy wait until 1 year before introducing whole egg |

| FOOD | 4-6 MONTHS | 6 MONTHS+ | 8 MONTHS+ | 10 MONTHS+ | 1 YEAR+ | NOTE |
|---|---|---|---|---|---|---|
| Citrus | No | No | No | No | After 1 year | |
| Nuts, peanuts, and peanut butter | No | No | No | No | Introduce as ground nuts and monitor for reaction | If risk of allergy, wait until 3 or 4 years. No whole nuts, pieces of nut or peanut butter until 5 as risk of choking |
| Sesame seeds and products | No | No | No | No | After 1 year and check for reaction | |
| Honey | No | No | No | No | After 1 year | |
| Tofu | No | No | Toward the end of this stage | | | |
| Berry fruits | No | Can be introduced mashed and pureed | | | | If risk of allergy wait until 1 year before introducing strawberries |
| Soft ripened cheeses | No | No | No | No | No | Introduce gradually |
| High-fiber foods | No | No | No | No | No | From 5 as part of a balanced diet |
| Tea and coffee, sodas and other adult drinks | No | No | No | No | No | To be avoided in child's diet |
| Salt | No | No | No | No | No | No need to add extra salt |
| Sugar | No | No | No | No | To be avoided except as part of cooking | |
| Artificial sweeteners, additives, etc. | No | No | No | No | No | To be avoided in child's diet |
| Wheat and wheat products | No | No | In moderation and gradually. Check for adverse reaction | | | |

# How Much is a Serving?

All babies and toddlers are different, so be guided by your own child's appetite. One to two year olds need the same variety and number of servings as older children but may need fewer calories, so offer smaller portions. You don't have to worry if your child does not eat the suggested servings every single day; it is what the child eats over a period of two to three weeks that counts. The following is a guide to standard portion sizes for children one to three years and older, but remember this is only a guide and children's appetites vary enormously.

Foods are divided into five main groups and there is a different daily need for each. Starchy carbohydrates, such as bread, rice, pasta, cereals, grains, and potatoes, should be served six times daily. At least half of these servings should be whole grains because they are more nutritious than processed varieties.

**✳ GRAINS, CEREALS, BREAD, ETC.:**
- ✳ ½–1 slice bread
- ✳ 1–2 tablespoons breakfast cereal
- ✳ 1–2 tablespoons cooked rice or pasta
- ✳ 1–2 tablespoons cooked porridge
- ✳ 1 small potato

Vegetables should be served three times a day. Serve a wide range of vegetables from orange fleshed, such as carrots and squash, and dark green, such as broccoli and spinach, through to starchy and leguminous varieties, such as peas and beans.
Fruits should be served twice a day. Try to give your baby a wide variety of fruits to obtain a balance of vitamins and minerals. Be careful when buying fruit juices and fruit

snacks, because these products often do not contain much real fruit. Fruit yogurts often contain little fruit and a lot of sugar, so it is better to serve plain yogurt with fresh fruit.

**✳ VEGETABLES AND FRUITS:**
- ✳ ½–1 medium apple, pear, or orange
- ✳ 1–2 tablespoons grapes or berries
- ✳ ½–1 kiwi, plum, or apricot
- ✳ 1–2 tablespoons stewed or canned fruit
- ✳ ½–1 tablespoon dried fruit
- ✳ ½–1 small carrot
- ✳ 1–2 tablespoons peas
- ✳ 1–2 florets broccoli or cauliflower

There should be two servings daily from meat, poultry, fish, eggs, nuts, and beans. Try to choose lean cuts of meat and limit fried foods—broiling or oven cooking is preferable.

**✻ MEAT, FISH, EGGS, ETC.:**
✻ 1–2 oz/25–55 g (½–1 slice) lean meat
✻ 1–2 oz/25–55 g poultry or fish
✻ ½–1 egg
✻ 1–2 tablespoons beans or lentils

Milk, yogurt, cheese, and other dairy products should be served 2–3 times a day. Children under 2 years need whole milk.

**✻ DAIRY PRODUCTS:**
✻ ⅔–¾ cup milk
✻ 1–1½ oz/25–40 g hard cheese
✻ 1–2 small (4½ oz/125 g) containers yogurt

Many foods, such as milk, nuts, and fruit, contain fats and sugars. There is no need to add to this with cakes, cookies, candies, jam, and sodas. All these foods should be served only as occasional treats.

# Milk & Drinks

Breast milk is the ideal food for babies in the first few months and indeed in the first year. Infant formula is fine up to one year. Soy milk may be prescribed if a child is intolerant to formula milk, however, soy, goat's and sheep's milk are not suitable for children under one year.

Remember that milk is a food and often your baby will just be thirsty. Water is the best thing to offer, and for babies under six months, use boiled and cooled tap water. Avoid bottled waters as these often have a high mineral and sodium content.

Soda, flavored milk, and juice drinks are unsuitable for babies and young children, because they contain sugar.

Well-diluted (one part juice to ten parts water), noncitrus fruit juice can be given at meal times to babies under a year. Citrus juices, again, well-diluted, can be given after a child's first birthday. Caffeine-rich drinks should never be given to babies or young children.

# Cooking, Freezing & Reheating

In the early days of weaning, babies eat very tiny amounts, so it is convenient to freeze individual portions of food. After preparing, let purees cool and then spoon into sections of an ice-cube tray or small plastic containers. Before six months it is best to sterilize these trays, but after that simply wash thoroughly in very hot water and scald with boiling water just before you use them. Freeze, and when solid, pop the cubes into a plastic container and label clearly with the type of food and the date.

When you want to use them, place in a small bowl, cover, and let thaw at room temperature for an hour or so, or for longer in the refrigerator. Always reheat thawed food thoroughly and then let it cool to the required temperature.

Baby foods heat quickly in the microwave, so heat in bursts of 10 seconds, stirring well to prevent hot spots from uneven heating. You may notice that the frozen food is a little dry, so add some boiled water to keep the food from scorching. Make sure the food you offer the baby is not too hot.

Always be careful with infant rice, cooked rice left at room temperature for several hours can cause food poisoning. Make small amounts of rice each time you need to and refrigerate any leftovers. Use within eight hours or freeze for up to two weeks.

# Allergies & Intolerances

Some children are more susceptible than others to a reaction triggered by certain foods. A bad reaction to a food, which leads to adverse symptoms but does not involve the immune system, is called food intolerance. A food allergy is different because it involves a fast response by the body's immune system, when antibodies are released to fight off the presence of the "intruder" food.

If there is a family history of allergy, it is advisable to breast-feed for at least four months and longer if possible; weaning should not occur before six months and introduce new foods one at a time.

Talk to your doctor if you are unable to breast-feed. When breastfeeding, monitor your diet because allergens can be passed through breast milk.

### ✳ SYMPTOMS OF FOOD INTOLERANCE:
✳ Skin rashes—eczema and hives
✳ Ear infections or asthma
✳ Bloating, excessive gas, or diarrhea
✳ Runny nose and coldlike symptoms
✳ Red puffy eyes and eyelids
✳ Nausea and vomiting

### ✳ SYMPTOMS OF FOOD ALLERGY:
✳ Severe breathing problems, coughs, and wheezing
✳ Swelling of lips, eyes, and tongue
✳ Increase in vomiting
✳ Blistering in or around the mouth
✳ Skin rashes or hives
✳ Bloating and excessive diarrhea

### ✳ FOODS THAT CAN CAUSE ADVERSE REACTIONS INCLUDE:
✳ Gluten, found in wheat, rye, oats, and barley
✳ Eggs, especially the whites
✳ Sesame seeds and products, such as tahini
✳ Nuts, especially peanuts
✳ Citrus fruit, such as oranges and lemons
✳ Kiwi
✳ Fish, especially shellfish
✳ Cow's milk and products made from cow's milk
✳ Soy
✳ Strawberries
✳ Tomatoes
✳ Chocolate
✳ Artificial additives, chemicals, preservatives, or dyes

Other foods to avoid giving your baby are salt, sugar, and honey. Honey can harbor the spores of *clostridium botulinum*. An adult's digestive system can deal with these spores, but in a baby the spores can grow and, produce life-threatening toxins.

Refer to the chart on pages 8–9 for the best age at which to introduce these foods. If you are at all worried about this, or if you have a history of food allergies, always consult your doctor.

# First Tastes 6-8 Months

There is no magic age or weight that will help you to decide when your baby is ready for weaning. The World Health Organization used to recommend that babies should be exclusively breast-fed until the age of six months. More recent advice, however, is that infants should not be given solids before four months and that a mixed diet should be given by six months. The timing and rate of introduction of solids will nevertheless depend very much on the individual.

Some mothers may be put under pressure to introduce solids too early. Before four to six months, babies' small intestines have large spaces between the cells to allow food molecules to pass directly into the blood. This allows large antibodies from breast milk to enter the bloodstream, but it also means that proteins from allergy-forming foods can pass through the intestines. At some point between four and six months, babies start producing their own antibodies and their kidneys become mature enough to cope with the waste products of solid food. This, therefore, is the best time to start solids.

✽ Some of the clues that your baby may be ready for weaning include:
✽ The baby sits well in a high chair and the head is held up well
✽ Is still hungry after eight to ten feedings of breast milk or 30 oz/850 g formula a day and demands feeds more often
✽ Used to sleep all through the night but is now waking up
✽ Shows significant weight gain (baby's birth weight has doubled)
✽ Makes chewing motions and is losing the tendency to push food out of the mouth with the tongue
✽ Can move food from the front to the back of the mouth
✽ Seems interested in food when you are eating

Up until now your baby's food has been only milk, so the first solid you give should be a go-between food that is really a thickened milk, because the process of swallowing solids has to be mastered slowly. Remember that during weaning, milk should still be the main food, with solids as an extra. Rice cereal mixed with milk is overwhelmingly recommended as a baby's first food because it is very bland and gluten-free, and it has the right consistency.

Make sure the infant rice is just lukewarm and the consistency of thin cream. Use a shallow plastic or rubber baby spoon and put just a quarter of a teaspoon of rice cereal on the tip. Allow the baby's mouth to open and just touch the spoon to the lips. Don't force the spoon into the mouth. Some babies are more comfortable sucking from your clean finger. Try this two or three times and then wait until the next day to try again.

Never put rice cereal into a bottle with milk, because this could cause choking. For the same reason, you should always feed your baby in an upright position. Bacteria can quickly grow in uneaten cereal or puree, so don't be tempted to leave it on the side in order to try again later—throw it away and make a fresh batch the next day to offer your baby.

It's important to offer the baby solids at the same time each day. Make sure you are not rushed and your baby is not tired or too hungry. Midmorning or lunchtime is a good time, and if you offer a little milk first it will curb any hunger pangs.

Once the baby gets the hang of swallowing and begins to enjoy the infant rice, gradually thicken the consistency and offer it twice a day. Over the next few weeks slowly introduce some vegetable and fruit purees, maybe mixing them in with a little rice at first. Wait three days before you introduce any new foods to check for any allergic reaction. Remember that weaning should be a very gradual process.

# Infant rice & first Purées

### HOMEMADE INFANT RICE
*2 tbsp brown rice*

*⅔ cup water*

*4–6 tbsp breast or formula milk,
plus extra for mixing*

***SERVINGS: 16***

### CARROT PUREE
*1 medium carrot, about
3½ oz/100 g*

***SERVINGS: 1–6***

### POTATO & TURNIP PUREE
*1 small potato
or sweet potato*

*1 small turnip*

***SERVINGS: 1–6***

## HOMEMADE INFANT RICE
**PREPARE: 5 MINUTES**
**COOK: 20 MINUTES**

✳ Grind the rice to a very fine powder in an electric grinder. Mix with the water in a small saucepan.

✳ Bring to a boil and simmer gently for 10 minutes, stirring continuously. By this stage, the rice will have thickened considerably.

✳ Stir in 4 tablespoons of the breast or formula milk and continue cooking, stirring continuously, for an additional 10 minutes. Add more milk if the mixture gets too thick.

✳ Remove from the heat and use a handheld electric blender to process the rice to a smooth, creamy puree. Cool the mixture. Just before offering it to the baby, add baby milk to thin it to the desired consistency. The temperature should be lukewarm.

**Store for up to 8 hours in the refrigerator or freeze for up to 2 weeks.**

## CARROT PUREE
**PREPARE: 3 MINUTES**
**COOK: 10 MINUTES**

✳ Peel the carrot. Chop into 1/8-inch/3-mm dice. Either steam in a metal steamer basket in a small saucepan or cook in enough unsalted boiling water just to cover for about 10 minutes, or until soft. Drain, reserving the cooking liquid.

✳ Puree using a handheld electric blender. Add 2–3 tablespoons of the hot cooking water or breast or formula milk and mix to a thin, slightly creamy consistency. Push through a fine strainer or through a food mill. Serve lukewarm.

**Store for 24 hours in the refrigerator or freeze for up to 4 weeks.**

## POTATO & TURNIP PUREE
**PREPARE: 5 MINUTES**
**COOK: 10–15 MINUTES**

✳ Peel and dice the vegetables and put them in a small saucepan with enough unsalted water to cover. Bring to a boil, cover, and simmer for 10–15 minutes, or until very tender. Drain, reserving the cooking liquid.

✳ To puree the vegetables, press them through a strainer or put them through a food mill, and add enough cooking water or baby's usual milk to thin to a smooth, creamy consistency. Serve lukewarm.

**Store for 24 hours in the refrigerator or freeze for up to 4 weeks.**

# Purees & Oatmeal Cereal

**SQUASH & SPINACH PUREE**
**PREPARE: 5 MINUTES**
**COOK: 20 MINUTES**
✳ Chop the butternut squash into small cubes. Put in a saucepan and add enough water to cover. Bring to a boil, then cover and simmer for 15 minutes. Add the spinach and cook for an additional 5 minutes. Drain, reserving the cooking liquid. Puree the mixture using a handheld electric blender. Add a little cooking liquid or baby's usual milk to thin. Serve lukewarm.
**Store for 24 hours in the refrigerator or freeze for up to 4 weeks.**

**OATMEAL CEREAL**
**PREPARE: 3 MINUTES**
**COOK: 5 MINUTES**
✳ Process the oats to a fine powder in an electric grinder. Put the water in a small saucepan and add the ground oats, mixing well. Bring to a boil, then simmer, stirring, for 3–5 minutes. Cool. Add breast or formula milk to thin. Add more milk, if necessary, as the cereal thickens on cooling. Serve lukewarm.
**Serve on day of making or freeze for up to 2 weeks.**

**APPLE & PEAR PUREE**
**PREPARE: 5 MINUTES**
**COOK: 10 MINUTES**
✳ Put all the ingredients in a small saucepan and bring to a boil. Cover and simmer for about 7–10 minutes, or until very soft. Check regularly that the fruit has not caught on the bottom of the saucepan.

---

**SQUASH & SPINACH PUREE**
¾ cup butternut squash, peeled and seeded
1 cup baby spinach leaves, washed

*SERVINGS: 1–6*

---

**OATMEAL CEREAL**
heaping ¼ cup rolled oats
generous ¾ cup water

*SERVINGS: 1–4*

---

**APPLE & PEAR PUREE**
1 apple, peeled, cored, and diced
1 pear, peeled, cored, and diced
3 tbsp water

*SERVINGS: 1–6*

19

# Pea, Bean & Zucchini Puree

**PREPARE: 5 MINUTES**
**COOK: 10 MINUTES**

✳ Put the beans and zucchini in a small saucepan with the peas and cover with unsalted boiling water.

✳ Simmer for 10 minutes, or until tender.

✳ Drain, reserving the cooking liquid.

✳ Puree using a handheld electric blender. Use a little cooking water to thin and then press through a strainer to remove any stringy parts or pea skins. Serve lukewarm. **Store for 24 hours in the refrigerator or freeze for up to 4 weeks.**

¼ *cup young, tender 1-inch/2.5-cm green bean pieces*

¼ *cup coarsely chopped zucchini*

¼ *cup fresh or frozen peas*

*SERVINGS: 1–6*

# Cauliflower & Broccoli Puree

**PREPARE: 5 MINUTES**
**COOK: 10 MINUTES**

✻ Coarsely chop the broccoli and cauliflower florets. Steam the florets for 7–10 minutes, until tender.

✻ Puree with a handheld electric blender until smooth. Alternatively, press the vegetables through a strainer or food mill.

✻ Add breast or formula milk to thin to a smooth, creamy puree. Serve lukewarm.
**Store for 24 hours in the refrigerator or freeze for up to 4 weeks.**

*3 small broccoli florets, hard stalks removed*

*3 small cauliflower florets, hard stalks removed*

*SERVINGS: 1-6*

# No-Cook Purees

## BANANA PUREE
**PREPARE: 5 MINUTES**

✳ Peel and mash half a small ripe banana with a fork then blend briefly using a handheld electric blender. Don't strain banana as the result is not good. Mix the puree with a little breast or formula milk if desired. Serve immediately.
**Do not refrigerate or freeze.**

## AVOCADO PUREE
**PREPARE: 5 MINUTES**

✳ Peel and remove the pit. Mash or puree one-quarter of the avocado. Mix with a little breast or formula milk to thin if desired. Serve immediately.
**Do not refrigerate or freeze.**

## MELON PUREE
**PREPARE: 5 MINUTES**

✳ Cut a small wedge of melon, scoop out the seeds, and remove the skin. Cut the flesh into chunks and strain or puree. Serve immediately or keep in the refrigerator until required, but serve on day of making.
**Do not freeze.**

*BANANA PUREE*
*½ small ripe banana*

*AVOCADO PUREE*
*¼ ripe avocado*

*MELON PUREE*
*small wedge of melon*

*SERVINGS: 1–3*

# Apricot & Prune Puree

**PREPARE: 12 HOURS**
**COOK: 10 MINUTES**

✳ Discard the soaking water and cook the apricots and prunes in boiling unsalted water to cover for about 10 minutes, or until very tender.

✳ Drain. Press the mixture through a strainer to remove any skins. Mix with boiled water until a smooth creamy consistency is obtained. Serve lukewarm.
**Store for 24 hours in the refrigerator or freeze for up to 4 weeks.**

**NOTE**
Prunes are a natural laxative.

*6 dried apricots (unsulfured), soaked overnight*

*2–3 stoned prunes, soaked overnight*

*2–3 tbsp boiled unsalted water*

*SERVINGS: 1–3*

# Establishing Solids 8-10 Months

Once your baby is enjoying first tastes, you can gradually start to introduce a wider range of foods and increase the number of meals a day from one to two and then three. Some babies rapidly progress from purees to chunkier foods and are ready at seven months, while others take a little longer. Once your baby is eating three meals a day, the solids can be given first and the milk second.

The very first "lumpy" foods should contain pieces no bigger than ⅛ inch/3 mm. They should be soft enough to squash between the tongue and the roof of the mouth and swallow without chewing. Different textures, first ground and then chopped food, can be given as baby begins to chew. As with first tastes, introduce new foods one at a time with at least three days in between to make sure your baby has no allergic reaction to them.

Some babies start to put food into their mouths independently of you, and this should be encouraged because they may refuse food from the spoon and prefer to feed themselves. This is a good time to start giving a selection of bite-size finger food, so that baby can experiment with the new-found skills of picking up, biting, and chewing. Even when they don't have teeth, it's amazing how efficient their gums are. Good first finger foods to try include sticks of steamed vegetables or peeled and pitted raw fruit, lightly toasted bread, and rice cakes.

Signs that a baby is ready for finger foods are:

- Swallows food much more easily
- No longer pushes food out with the tongue
- Tries to use a spoon
- Uses the thumb and index finger to pick up food

As the baby becomes more interested in food and in feeding without your help, you need to watch out for foods that can be a choking hazard. Vegetables and fruits must be soft; any meat or poultry should be pureed or ground. Avoid raisins, popcorn, pieces of bread (unless very small), grapes, fries, and candies, and remember that whenever children are eating they should always be closely supervised.

You can start to give your baby some pureed or mashed family food, providing you make sure the food does not contain salt, too much fat, strong spices, or sugar, and is not likely to cause an allergic reaction. It is good to get your baby used to your cooking, and the social side of eating is a very important part of babies' development, so they should be allowed to join in as much as possible.

Commercial baby foods are useful to complement family and homecooked food, particularly when you are away from home or when time is short at home and your baby is very hungry. However, they should not replace freshly cooked food. If possible, choose organic baby food and make sure it does not contain added sugar, salt, artificial additives, thickeners, or fillers.

As more foods are introduced, babies will, of course, start to exert their independence and refuse both new foods and those they may have liked previously. It is sometimes difficult when you are in a rush or have spent time preparing food not to get annoyed at this stage. Forcing your baby to eat, however, will only lead to confrontation and frustration. If the baby refuses any food, just take it calmly away and offer it again another time. Don't be tempted to offer a sweet replacement because you are worried the baby is hungry. Babies will always eat when they are hungry. Our appetites vary from day to day and it's the same with babies; the only way they can communicate this to you is by refusing to eat, thus sending out the message "I'm not that hungry today." If you use food as a reward or a punishment, you will have trouble later on. Let mealtimes be about enjoyment and eating and nothing else.

# Creamy Tomato & Lentil Soup

**PREPARE: 10 MINUTES**
**COOK: 1 HOUR, 15 MINUTES**

✳ Put the lentils in a pan and cover with unsalted water, then bring to a boil. Reduce the heat and let simmer, partially covered, for 20–25 minutes, or until tender. Drain well and set aside.

✳ While the lentils are cooking, make the soup. Heat the oil in a heavy-bottom skillet. Add the onion, then cover and cook over low heat for 10 minutes, or until softened. Add the carrot and celery and cook for an additional 2 minutes, stirring occasionally to prevent the vegetables from sticking to the bottom of the skillet and burning. Add the creamed tomatoes and stock and bring to a boil. Reduce the heat and let simmer, partially covered, for 20–25 minutes, or until the vegetables are tender and the liquid has reduced and thickened.

✳ Add the lentils to the skillet. Carefully pour the mixture into a blender or food processor and blend until smooth and creamy. Swirl a spoonful of cream or yogurt, if using, over the soup and serve.

✳ For the Cheese Toasts, preheat the broiler to high. Lightly toast the bread fingers on one side. Butter the other side and sprinkle with the cheese, and oregano, if using. Broil until golden. Serve the soup lukewarm, with the cheese toasts for dipping.
**Store the soup for 24 hours in the refrigerator or freeze for up to 4 weeks.**

generous 2 tbsp red split lentils, rinsed

2 tsp olive oil

1 small onion, chopped

1 small carrot, peeled, and very finely chopped

1 small celery stalk, chopped

9 oz/250 g carton creamed tomatoes

1¼ cups unsalted or homemade vegetable stock

cream or plain yogurt, to serve (optional)

## CHEESE TOASTS

2 slices bread, cut into strips

butter, for spreading

¼ cup grated Gruyère or Cheddar cheese

pinch of dried oregano, (optional)

**SERVINGS: 4–6**

# Pasta with Butternut Squash

**PREPARE: 5 MINUTES**
**COOK: 15–20 MINUTES**

✳ Steam the butternut squash for about 10–15 minutes, or until tender, then puree or mash with a fork.

✳ Meanwhile, cook the pasta according to the package directions, then drain well and return to the pan. Add the butter, oil, and Parmesan cheese and stir until the pasta is coated, then combine with the butternut squash. Serve lukewarm and consume on day of making. **Do not refrigerate or freeze.**

*3 oz/85 g butternut squash, peeled, seeded, and chopped*

*½ cup dried baby pasta shapes or pastina*

*small piece of unsalted butter*

*1 tsp olive oil*

*1 tbsp freshly grated Parmesan cheese*

*SERVINGS: 1–3*

# Macaroni & Cheese

**PREPARE: 5 MINUTES**
**COOK: 25 MINUTES**

✳ Preheat the oven to 350°F/180°C. Cook the macaroni and peas, according to the package directions, in separate small saucepans.

✳ Drain. Mix together and put in a small baking dish. Pour over the sauce, stirring once to combine. Mix together the breadcrumbs and Parmesan cheese and sprinkle over the top.

✳ Arrange the tomatoes on top. Bake for 10 minutes. Mash or puree as desired. Serve lukewarm and consume on day of making. **Freeze for up to 4 weeks.**

2 oz/55 g dried whole wheat macaroni

4 tbsp frozen peas

scant ⅔ cup low-sodium store-bought cheese sauce

1 tbsp homemade fresh breadcrumbs

1 tbsp freshly grated Parmesan cheese

2 cherry tomatoes, sliced

*SERVINGS: 1–3*

# Baked Flounder with Tomato Rice

**PREPARE: 15 MINUTES**
**COOK: 40 MINUTES**

✳ Preheat the oven to 350°F/180°C. Put the flounder on a large piece of baking paper, brush with oil, and arrange the fresh tomatoes on top. Fold up the baking paper to make a parcel and encase the fish. Place the parcel on a baking sheet and bake in the preheated oven for 10 minutes.

✳ Meanwhile, put the rice and canned tomatoes in a saucepan and cover with the water. Bring to a boil, then reduce the heat, cover and simmer for 15 minutes. Add the herbs, carrot, and beans and simmer for an additional 10–15 minutes, or until the water has been absorbed.

✳ Remove the basil sprig. Remove the skin and any bones from the fish and flake the flesh. Fold the fish and fresh tomatoes into the tomato rice and serve pureed, mashed, or as it is, depending on the age of your baby. Serve on day of making.
**Do not freeze.**

1 small flounder fillet

olive oil, for brushing

2 tomatoes, peeled, seeded and coarsely chopped

3 oz/85 g brown long-grain rice, rinsed

4 tbsp canned chopped tomatoes

¾ cup unsalted water

1 sprig of fresh basil leaves

½ tsp dried oregano

1 small carrot, peeled and diced

3 fine French beans, sliced

*SERVINGS: 1–3*

# Spring Vegetable Rice

**PREPARE: 10 MINUTES**
**COOK: 40 MINUTES**

✻ Steam the leek and zucchini for 2 minutes, then add the peas and cook for 3 minutes.

✻ Melt the butter with the oil in a heavy-bottom skillet. Add the rice and cook, stirring, for 2–3 minutes, or until the grains are well coated in the butter and oil and are translucent.

✻ Add the stock a ladleful at a time, waiting until it has been absorbed before adding more.

*½ small leek, peeled and very finely chopped*

*½ small zucchini, very finely chopped*

*small handful of frozen peas*

*small piece of unsalted butter*

*1 tsp olive oil*

*¼ cup risotto rice*

*¾ cup hot low-sodium or homemade vegetable or chicken stock*

*½ tsp dried oregano*

*1 tbsp freshly grated Parmesan cheese*

**SERVINGS: 1–3**

✻ Cook over medium-low heat for 20 minutes, stirring continuously. Add the oregano, Parmesan cheese, and vegetables and let simmer, stirring, for an additional 5–10 minutes, or until all the liquid has been absorbed, and the rice is tender. Puree the risotto, mash it, or leave it as it is, depending on your baby's age, adding extra stock or water if it is too thick. Serve on day of making.
**Do not freeze.**

# Chicken, Leek & Mushroom Casserole

**PREPARE: 10 MINUTES**
**COOK: 25 MINUTES**

✳ Heat the oil in a small saucepan and gently cook the leek and chicken for 8–10 minutes, until the leek is tender and the chicken is cooked but not browned. Add the mushrooms, potato, and apple.

✳ Add the stock, cover, and simmer gently for about 15 minutes, until the vegetables are tender.

✳ Puree, mash, or serve as it is, depending on the age of your baby.
**Store for up to 24 hours in the refrigerator or freeze for up to 4 weeks.**

*2 tsp olive oil*

*1 oz/25 g leek, finely chopped*

*2 oz/55 g chicken breast, cut into small dice*

*1 oz/25 g white mushrooms, finely chopped*

*1 oz/25 g potato or sweet potato, peeled and chopped*

*¼ small apple, peeled, cored, and chopped*

*⅔ cup low-sodium or homemade chicken stock*

**SERVINGS: 1–3**

# Lamb with Apricots

**PREPARE: 5 MINUTES**
**COOK: 25 MINUTES**

✳ Heat the oil in a saucepan. Add the lamb and onion and cook for 2–3 minutes, until lightly browned. Add the potato, carrot, apricots, stock, and tomato paste. Cover and simmer very gently for 10–15 minutes. Using a food processor or handheld electric blender, blend to the desired consistency.

✳ Put the couscous into a bowl and pour over the boiling water. Let stand for 5 minutes and then fluff up the grains with a fork. Stir the couscous into the lamb and serve lukewarm. Serve on day of making.

**Freeze the lamb mixture, without the couscous, for up to 4 weeks.**

*1 tsp vegetable oil*

*2 oz/55 g lean ground lamb*

*2 tsp finely chopped onion*

*2 oz/55 g potato, peeled and diced*

*2 oz/55 g carrot, diced*

*1–2 plumped dried apricots, chopped*

*⅔ cup low-sodium or homemade vegetable stock*

*1 tsp tomato paste*

*2 tbsp couscous*

*generous ⅓ cup unsalted boiling water*

**SERVINGS: 1–3**

# Apple & Plum Yogurt

**PREPARE: 5 MINUTES**
**COOK: 10 MINUTES**

✳ Put the apple and plums in a saucepan with the water. Bring to a boil, then reduce the heat and simmer, covered, for 5 minutes, or until tender. Remove the plum skins and puree the fruit in a blender or press through a sieve until smooth.

✳ Mix the fruit puree and yogurt together, then sprinkle over the crushed cookie, if using, before serving. **Store for 24 hours in the refrigerator but do not freeze.**

*1 small dessert apple, peeled, cored, and chopped*

*2 ripe plums, stoned*

*2 tbsp water*

*4–6 tbsp plain yogurt*

*1 plain cookie, crushed (optional)*

**SERVINGS: 2**

# Experimenting with Tastes
## 10-16 Months

As your baby reaches ten months of age, you will find that meal options increase. Babies of this age can handle new tastes and textures, and their interest in feeding themselves can be encouraged by offering a wide range of tasty finger foods and allowing them to experiment with using a spoon.

From around nine to ten months old, babies become more interested in feeding themselves, and will want to hold a spoon as well as eating with their fingers. From day to day babies develop at an incredibly rapid rate. They can be very active and, although their energy and protein requirements are high in relation to their size, their appetites may still be small.

You can now start to introduce stronger flavors, but do this gradually, and watch for any allergic reaction. A balanced diet for your child will include breads and cereals, lean meat, poultry, dairy products, beans and lentils, and plenty of fruits and vegetables. As they eat more solids, the child will also need less milk. Although milk is still important, much of their calcium can now come from whole dairy products such as cheese, yogurt, milky desserts, and sauces, as well as from vegetables, such as broccoli.

For toddlers, you may be aware that your child, who was once happy to eat anything, can now become grouchy and obstinate, refusing even foods which were once their favorites.

Here are some tips to ensure mealtimes are peaceful affairs, and eating is enjoyable and fun.

✲ **TIPS ON ENJOYABLE AND PEACEFUL MEALTIMES:**
✲ One way to introduce new foods is to mix them in with foods you know the child likes. Unpopular vegetables can be hidden in soup or pasta sauces.
✲ Ensure your child has plenty of fresh air and exercise so they are hungry when they eat.
✲ Serve small portions and don't insist that your child finishes everything on the plate—a little food is better than nothing.
✲ Don't offer snacks too close to meal times.
✲ When possible, allow him or her to help with shopping and preparation—from putting apples in a bag at the supermarket to then placing them in a bowl once at home.
✲ Try to ensure your child doesn't eat alone. If you or your family are busy eating, then your child will follow suit.
✲ Never bargain with food. Make no fuss but simply remove the food and offer something healthy, such as fruit, until the next meal or snack.
✲ If a food is rejected, simply remove and try again at another time. Remember, the refusal to eat could be due to a number of causes, including teething, sickness, or tiredness. It may also take two or three attempts before a new food is accepted.
✲ Allow the child to choose sometimes. Would they prefer a banana or an apple?
✲ Remember: children never starve themselves!

Up until now your child's diet has mainly depended on breast or formula milk. From the age of one babies can be given whole cow's (or goat or sheep's) milk, about 1½ cups a day, as part of a well-balanced diet. Make the changeover slowly, especially if you are breastfeeding.

Keep in mind that a child under five has different nutritional needs to older children and adults. They need more fat and calories and less fiber. The fat and calories assist in the growth of the brain and nervous system. Without enough fat and calories to burn, the body will burn protein instead and protein is needed to build muscle. To keep their blood sugar up, toddlers need to eat and drink every two to three hours. So, although we are conditioned to eat just three meals a day, what a toddler needs is three small meals with the addition of healthy, nutritious snacks in between.

# Breadsticks with Dips

**NO-SALT BREADSTICKS**
¾ cup white bread flour

¾ cup whole wheat bread flour

¼-oz/7-g sachet active dry yeast
(about 1 level tsp)

1 tbsp olive oil

about ¾ cup lukewarm water
(mix one-third boiling water with
two-thirds cold)

**SERVINGS: ABOUT 60 SMALL
BREADSTICKS**

**NO-SALT BREADSTICKS**
**PREPARE: 15 MINUTES**
**COOK: 10 MINUTES**

✱ Preheat the oven to 425°F/220°C. Put the flours and yeast into a bowl
and add the olive oil and enough water to mix to a soft but not sticky dough.
Knead for about 5 minutes, until smooth and elastic. Divide the dough into
4 pieces.

✱ Roll each piece out to a long, very thin sausage and cut into small sticks
about 3 inches/ 7 cm long. Place on a nonstick baking sheet and bake for
about 7–10 minutes, until golden and crisp. Serve with the dips.
**Store for up to 2 weeks in an airtight container.**

## HUMMUS
### PREPARE: 10 MINUTES

\* It's worth making your own hummus for baby because prepared versions can be salty and contain tahini, a sesame seed-based paste, which can very occasionally cause an allergic reaction and is best given when your child is older.

\* Put all the ingredients into a food processor and blend until smooth. Add a little more lemon juice or yogurt to taste, if desired.
**Store for up to 3 days in the refrigerator.**

## AVOCADO DIP
### PREPARE: 5 MINUTES

\* Mash the avocado with a fork and mix in the lemon juice and yogurt.
**Store for up to 2 days in the refrigerator.**

## BEET DIP
### PREPARE: 15 MINUTES
### COOK: 15 MINUTES

\* Cut the beet into very small dice and cook in a little boiling water for 12–15 minutes, until soft. Cool. Peel and coarsely grate the apple. Put the beet, apple, lemon juice, and sour cream into a bowl and process until smooth using a handheld electric blender.
**Store for up to 2 days in the refrigerator.**

---

### HUMMUS
*14 oz/400 g canned unsweetened, low-sodium chickpeas, drained and rinsed*

*1 garlic clove*

*1 tbsp olive oil*

*a little freshly squeezed lemon or lime juice*

*1 tbsp plain yogurt*

*SERVINGS: 10–15*

---

### AVOCADO DIP
*½ ripe avocado*

*1 tsp lemon juice*

*2–3 tsp plain yogurt*

*SERVINGS: 1–6*

---

### BEET DIP
*1 small fresh beet, peeled*

*½ small apple*

*squeeze of lemon juice*

*1 tbsp sour cream or plain yogurt*

*SERVINGS: 1–10*

# Pasta with Red Bell Pepper Sauce

**PREPARE: 30 MINUTES**
**(EXCLUDING COOLING TIME FOR PEPPER)**
**COOK: 40 MINUTES**

✳ Preheat the oven to 400°F/200°C. Put the bell pepper on a baking sheet and drizzle with half the oil. Roast for about 20–25 minutes, until soft and blackened. Put into a large plastic bag and seal the top. Let stand until cold. The steam created in the bag helps to separate the skin from the flesh of the pepper. Peel the pepper and remove the stalk and seeds. Puree using a food processor or handheld electric blender.

✳ Heat the remaining oil in a small saucepan and cook the shallot and garlic gently for about 5 minutes. Meanwhile, cook the pasta in a separate saucepan, according to the package directions.

✳ Add the red pepper puree, stock, butternut squash, and chicken to the shallot and garlic. Heat gently for about 5 minutes, adding more stock if necessary. Drain the pasta and add to the red pepper mixture. Toss well and serve sprinkled with the parsley.
**Do not refrigerate or freeze.**

*1 red bell pepper, halved*

*2 tbsp olive oil*

*1 small shallot, finely chopped*

*1 garlic clove, crushed or very finely chopped*

*½ cup mini pasta shapes*

*3–6 tbsp water or low-sodium chicken or vegetable stock*

*1 tbsp cooked butternut squash, mashed or chopped*

*2 oz/55 g cooked chicken breast, chopped or ground*

*1 tsp finely chopped fresh parsley*

*SERVINGS: 1–2*

# Falafel with Carrot Salad

**PREPARE: 15 MINUTES**
**COOK: 5 MINUTES**

✳ Put the chickpeas, onion, spices, herbs, and flour into a food processor and blend until smooth. With lightly floured hands, shape the mixture into small patties.

✳ Heat a little sunflower oil in a skillet and when hot, cook the falafel for 2–3 minutes on each side, turning only once during cooking. Drain the falafel on paper towels.

✳ Mix together the carrot, apple, raisins, lemon juice, and mint. Serve the falafel with a little of this salad, a spoonful of yogurt, and 2–3 strips of pita bread.

**Store for 24 hours in the refrigerator or freeze for up to 4 weeks.**

*14 oz/400 g canned unsweetened, low-sodium chickpeas, drained and rinsed*

*¼ small onion*

*1 tsp ground coriander*

*1 tsp ground cumin*

*1 tbsp chopped fresh parsley*

*1 tbsp chopped fresh cilantro*

*2 tbsp whole wheat flour, plus extra for dusting*

*sunflower oil, for cooking*

*FOR SERVING:*

*1 medium carrot, coarsely grated*

*½ apple, peeled and coarsely grated*

*2 tbsp raisins, chopped*

*1 tsp lemon juice*

*1 tsp chopped fresh mint*

*2–3 tbsp Greek-style yogurt*

*strips of pita bread*

*MAKES: 8–10 FALAFEL*

# Cheesy Corn Fritters

**PREPARE: 10 MINUTES**
**COOK: 10 MINUTES**

✳ Put the egg and milk into a small bowl and beat with a fork. Add the flour and baking powder and beat until smooth. Stir in the corn, cheese, and chives. Heat a little sunflower oil in a skillet and drop either teaspoonfuls or tablespoonfuls of the batter into it. Cook for 1–2 minutes on each side, until the fritters are puffed up and golden.

✳ Drain on paper towels and serve with extra corn and mini carrot sticks.
**Do not freeze.**

1 egg

generous ¾ cup milk

¾ cup all-purpose flour

½ tsp baking powder

⅓ cup unsweetened, low-sodium canned corn kernels, drained

4 tbsp grated cheddar cheese

1 tsp snipped fresh chives

2 tsp sunflower oil, for frying

*FOR SERVING*

extra corn kernels

mini carrot sticks

*MAKES: 4–6 LARGE OR 8–10 SMALL FRITTERS*

# Mini Meatballs & Spaghetti

**PREPARE: 10 MINUTES**
**COOK: 15 MINUTES**

✳ To make the meatballs, put the ground meat, onion, basil, and breadcrumbs into a small bowl and process using a handheld electric blender. Divide and shape the mixture into even bite-size balls.

✳ Heat the oil in a small saucepan and cook the meatballs, turning frequently, for 2–3 minutes, until lightly browned. Pour over the pasta sauce, cover, and simmer gently for about 10 minutes.

✳ Cook the spaghetti in a separate saucepan, according to the package directions. Drain. Serve the spaghetti topped with the meatballs and sauce. Sprinkle with parsley, if liked.

**Freeze the meatballs and sauce for up to 4 weeks.**

*2 oz/55 g lean ground beef*

*1 tsp finely chopped onion*

*2 tsp chopped fresh basil*

*1 tbsp homemade fresh whole wheat breadcrumbs*

*1 tsp olive oil*

*scant ½ cup store-bought, low-sodium tomato pasta sauce*

*2 oz/55 g dried spaghetti, broken into short lengths*

*finely chopped fresh parsley (optional)*

***MAKES: 8–10 MEATBALLS***

# Chicken Quesadilla Triangles

**PREPARE: 10 MINUTES**
**COOK: 10 MINUTES**

✳ Preheat the oven to 400°F/200°C. Lightly brush one tortilla with a little melted butter and place, butter side down, on a baking sheet. Arrange the chicken, cheese, and tomato over the tortilla, leaving a gap around the edge.

✳ Place the second tortilla on top and brush with the remaining butter. Bake for about 10 minutes, until the cheese has melted and the top is brown.

✳ Let cool slightly then cut into triangles and serve with sour cream.
**Do not refrigerate or freeze.**

2 small (8-inch/20-cm) flour tortillas

1–2 tsp melted butter, for brushing

½ small cooked skinless, boneless chicken breast, finely chopped

¾ cup grated cheddar cheese (or a mixture of cheddar cheese and mozzarella cheese)

1 tomato, peeled, seeded, and diced

*FOR SERVING*

2 tsp sour cream, seasoned with a squeeze of lime juice and a little chopped cilantro

*SERVINGS: 1–2*

# Sweet-&-Sour Chicken Stir-Fry

**PREPARE: 10 MINUTES**
**COOK: 10 MINUTES**

✳ Cook or soak the noodles according to the package directions. Heat the oil in a wok and stir-fry the chicken until lightly browned and cooked through. Add the carrot, baby corn, sugar snap peas, pineapple, and scallions and cook for 1–2 minutes. Add the bok choy, pineapple juice, soy sauce, and vinegar and stir together until the bok choy has just wilted.

✳ Drain the noodles and serve topped with the chicken and vegetables. Add a little more soy sauce, if liked.
**Do not refrigerate or freeze.**

2 oz/55 g medium egg noodles

1 tbsp vegetable oil

2 oz/55 g skinless, boneless chicken breast, cut into thin strips

½ small carrot, cut into matchsticks

2 baby corn, halved widthwise and lengthwise

4 sugar snap peas, cut into strips

2 oz/55 g pineapple, chopped

2 scallions, sliced

1 oz/25 g bok choy or baby spinach, coarsely torn

1 tsp pineapple juice

1 tsp lite soy sauce

1 tsp rice or sherry vinegar

FOR SERVING
soy sauce (optional)

SERVINGS: 2